MY FAMILY REMEMBERS

The 1970s

Kath Walker

W

Franklin Watts
This edition published in Great Britain in 2015
by The Watts Publishing Group

Planned and produced by Discovery Books Ltd., 2 College Street,
Ludlow, Shropshire, SY8 1AN
www.discoverybooks.net
Editor: James Nixon
Design: Blink Media

Words that are **bold** in the text are explained in the glossary.

Dewey number: 941

ISBN: 978 1 4451 4355 2

Printed in China

Franklin Watts
An imprint of
Hachette Children's Group
Part of The Watts Publishing Group
Carmelite House
50 Victoria Embankment
London EC4Y 0DZ

An Hachette UK Company
www.hachette.co.uk

www.franklinwatts.co.uk

Words that are **bold** in the text are explained in the glossary.

Contents

Meet the families

The 1970s was a decade of important changes. At the start of the decade, the age when young people could vote and marry without their parents' permission dropped from 21 to 18.

The '70s ended with another big change when Margaret Thatcher became Britain's first woman prime minister. Four children's families share their memories of those days.

Alice

Alice's family

Alice Hibberd is 13 years old. She has an older sister called Meg and lives with her mother, Julie, and stepfather, Tony. Julie was born in 1959 and was aged 10 at the start of the 1970s.

Julie

Sarah

Sarah's family

Sarah Hadland is 12 years old and lives with her older brother, Jacob, and parents, Marcia and Dan. Marcia was born in 1967 and aged between 3 and 13 in the '70s while Dan, who was born in 1971, was aged between 1 and 8.

Marcia

Dan

Matty

Hazel

Matty's family

Matty Morris is 12 years old. He lives with his younger sister, Milly, his older brother, Peter, and his parents, Julie and Kevin. Karen is Matty's aunt and was born in 1967. She was aged between 3 and 13 in the 1970s.

Hazel's family

Hazel Stancliffe is 11 years old. She lives with her older sister, Lily, and her parents, Abigail and Paul. Abigail was born in 1967 and was aged between 3 and 13 in the 1970s, while Paul was born in 1965 and aged between 5 and 15.

Karen

Paul

Abigail

Gloom and glitter

The 1970s was a difficult time for Britain. Prices rose and many workers went on **strike**. Some of the strikes caused **power cuts** which lasted for hours at a time. Also, the **Troubles** in Northern Ireland turned very violent. Bombs set off both there and in England killed and injured ordinary people as well as soldiers.

In 1972, a bomb was planted by an Irish terrorist group at this British army building in Aldershot, England. Seven people died in the explosion.

Alice asks her mother about the bombings:

I was in London at the Motor Show when there was a **bomb scare** and everyone had to leave the building quickly. Out on the street there were crowds of people and I got separated from my friends. It was really scary.

But it wasn't all gloom. Fashion and music brought lots of colour and glitter. It was a decade of disco dancing, strange hairstyles and **punk**.

There was a craze for disco music and dancing in nightclubs during the 1970s.

Sarah asks her mother about the '70s:
The amazing summer of 1976 was the hottest and longest that people could remember. We put our tents up in the garden and camped out.

This picture was taken during the long, hot summer of 1976. You can see that the grass has been scorched brown by the sun.

In 1977, Britain marked 25 years of the Queen's **reign** with the **Silver Jubilee** celebrations. There were street parties and parades throughout the country.

A special set of stamps was released for the Silver Jubilee.

Hazel asks her mother about the Queen's Silver Jubilee:
The Silver Jubilee was a really happy day. All the neighbours got together to celebrate with a street party. There were lines of tables in the street and ladies bustling about pouring out drinks.

Two children wearing party hats and carrying flags make their way to a Silver Jubilee street party in June 1977.

Life at home

Housework was getting easier in the 1970s as more homes had gadgets such as food mixers, freezers and dishwashers. Then in the late '70s, the first microwave cookers went on sale. Even making the beds got easier as people started to use duvets instead of sheets and blankets.

A modern 1970s kitchen had cupboards and a sink fitted to the walls like these.

There were new types of **convenience food** on sale that took just minutes to prepare, so people spent less time cooking. Also, people were eating out more often or buying takeaways. The number of Indian restaurants and places selling fast food quickly grew. The first McDonald's in the UK opened in 1974.

Hazel asks her father about his house:
Until I was 12, we lived in a small terraced house without a bathroom. The toilet was at the bottom of the garden and it often froze up in the winter. We moved in 1974 when the houses were knocked down to make way for a supermarket.

Get the best of the hot and cold. At McDonald's.

The best of both are as close as your nearby McDonald's. Hot and hearty Big Mac," famous for its seven great ingredients... one great taste.

And the tingling cold refreshment of Coca-Cola: After all, one good thing deserves another. You deserve a break today"

McDonald's
We do it all for you.

Here is an advert for McDonald's in 1975.

TIME DIFFERENCE

In 1979, 55 per cent of all British homes had central heating and 69 per cent had a telephone. Now, about 95 per cent of homes have central heating and 90 per cent have a telephone.

Big, chunky furniture made of wood, leather and steel was fashionable in the '70s, and thick **shagpile carpet** gave many homes a look of luxury. Browns, oranges and creams were very popular colours for walls and fabrics.

Matty's aunt (left) at home in her living room in the 1970s with her mother and sister.

Sarah asks her mother how life at home was different:
The street we grew up in was a lot quieter in the '70s than it is now – there was hardly any traffic on it then. People didn't have to worry about locking things up like they do today. We left the back door open most of the time.

Bold, striped patterns were popular coverings for sofas and chairs in the '70s.

Going shopping

During the '70s, there were big changes in the ways people shopped. With lots of big, new supermarkets opening, fewer shoppers bought their food from the small shops. Many local stores had to close down.

This big Sainsbury's supermarket formed part of a new shopping centre in Derby when it opened in 1975.

People were buying more ready-made meals that you heated up in the oven. Also popular were powdered soups, puddings and mashed potatoes that you prepared by just adding water.

Matty asks his aunt about shopping:

Mum shopped locally for fresh food, but once a week she would go to a big supermarket in Worcester. This was mainly for tinned food to store in the cupboard. She also bought some convenience foods and my favourite was Vesta Beef Curry (right).

Curry on eating.

We should have called it 'Kari' (that's where our word 'curry' came from) because of its very real Indian touches: a hint of apple, a handful of sultanas, beef and rice.

And herbs and spices from the East: coriander, cardamon, fenugreek and cumin. Real 'Kari' taste.

Vesta Beef Curry. Try it. You'll see what we mean.

VESTA Beef Curry & Rice

Have a change, for a change. Vesta.

There was much more interest in foreign foods in the '70s and new items, such as pasta, peppers and olive oil, appeared on the supermarket shelves.

TIME DIFFERENCE

In the 1970s, supermarkets offered about 5,000 different types of goods. Today's supermarkets offer about 40,000 different goods!

On 1 February 1971, the money that people used in Britain changed. The old system of pounds, **shillings** and pence was replaced by the **decimal** system we use today. The new money was simpler but many older people found the change difficult.

This is a set of the first British decimal coins. The halfpenny (bottom-centre) is no longer in use. The fifty, ten and five pence pieces were larger then and there was not a twenty pence coin.

Hazel asks her father about decimalisation:

There was a big build-up to 'Decimalisation Day' and at school they were busy teaching us the new system. I was very sad that the threepenny bit [a coin worth just over 1p] would no longer exist. This was my pocket money and lasted me a week in sweets.

Threepenny bit

Playtime

People did not have personal computers in the 1970s, but there were some exciting new types of home entertainment. In the early '70s, 'Pong' became one of the first home video games that you plugged into your television to play. It was an on-screen game of tennis and very simple compared to today's electronic games.

TV advertising encouraged crazes for toys such as Clackers. These were two hard balls on a string and the trick was to make them click together. Playgrounds were filled with the loud clacking sound until schools banned them for being too dangerous.

In Pong, each player turns a dial to move a paddle up and down vertically. The paddle blocks the ball and bounces it back to the opponent.

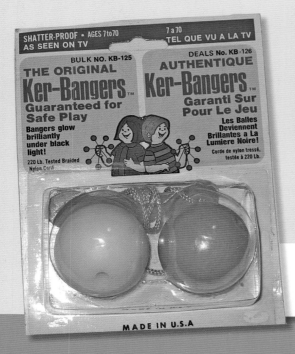

Hazel asks her father about toys in the '70s:
We only had a few toys, but we did have Clackers which could break your wrists if you weren't careful. My favourite games were the pretend games I used to play on the waste ground near my home. I used to pretend I was a wildlife film-maker in the desert.

Ker-Bangers, or Clackers, were very popular in the early '70s. They were banned in schools when a number of children were injured while playing with them.

The Raleigh Chopper was the 'must-have' children's bike of the '70s. It cost about £35, which was very expensive for the time.

In 1970, the Chopper bike was top of many kids' Christmas lists. It was made in the style of the American chopper motorcycle and was the coolest bike of its time. Later on in the '70s, a craze for skateboarding started and the first 'skate parks' opened.

Sarah asks her mother about having fun:

I used to play with my brothers a lot. My oldest brother had a Chopper bike when it was really something to have one. He used to give me 'backies' on it – where I would sit behind up on the back of the bike. It was very dangerous though.

This is a picture of Sarah's mother Marcia (left) and her two brothers taken in the 1970s.

At the movies

After watching the blockbuster movie *Jaws*, many children were terrified of swimming in the sea!

There were some huge '**blockbuster**' movies in the 1970s. Unlike movies before, these opened in hundreds of cinemas at the same time and were seen by massive audiences. The first of these was *Jaws* (1975), a film about a killer shark attacking swimmers. It had audiences on the edge of their seats.

The **science fiction** movie *Star Wars* in 1977 made more money than any film before it. Its dazzling space battles were thrilling, and its catchphrase 'May the Force be with you' became famous.

The terrifying motion picture from the terrifying No. 1 best seller.

JAWS

ROY SCHEIDER · ROBERT SHAW · RICHARD DREYFUSS

JAWS

Co-starring LORRAINE GARY · MURRAY HAMILTON · A ZANUCK/BROWN PRODUCTION
Screenplay by PETER BENCHLEY and CARL GOTTLIEB · Based on the novel by PETER BENCHLEY · Music by JOHN WILLIAMS
Directed by STEVEN SPIELBERG · Produced by RICHARD D. ZANUCK and DAVID BROWN · A UNIVERSAL PICTURE
TECHNICOLOR® PANAVISION® **PG** PARENTAL GUIDANCE SUGGESTED · ORIGINAL SOUNDTRACK AVAILABLE ON MCA RECORDS & TAPES ...MAY BE TOO INTENSE FOR YOUNGER CHILDREN

STAR WARS

Sarah asks her father what films he remembers best: When *Star Wars* came out it caused lots of excitement. Its special effects were incredible – we'd never seen anything like it before. It was something else!

John Travolta was the star of two hit movies: *Saturday Night Fever* (1977) and the musical *Grease* (1978). Music from both films topped the record charts and the amazing dance routines in *Saturday Night Fever* sparked a disco craze.

The film *Grease* was set in an American high school in the 1950s. The lead parts were played by John Travolta and singer Olivia Newton-John.

In the late '70s, video cassette recorders (VCRs) went on sale in UK shops. At first, VCRs were mainly for recording TV programmes, but they also allowed people to watch movies on video in their own homes.

Matty asks his aunt about her favourite films:
One of my favourite films of the time was *Grease*. I saw it eight times! I loved the clothes they wore and got to know all the songs.

Leisure time

By 1977, 66 per cent of homes had colour televisions while 31 per cent still had black and white. Unlike today, television broadcasting stopped at night and there were only three channels.

Programmes for younger children included the **animations** *Bagpuss, Clangers* and *The Wombles*. American puppet shows *Sesame Street* and the *Muppets* were also big TV hits. Police and detective shows were very popular in the '70s. Both adults and children enjoyed watching the American series *Hawaii Five-O* and *Starsky & Hutch*.

The Wombles was about a group of pointy-nosed creatures who lived in London's Wimbledon Common. Wombles cleared up rubbish left by humans and found good uses for it.

TIME DIFFERENCE
In 1971, a licence for a colour TV cost £12. Now it costs £149.

Sarah asks her father what he watched:

I liked watching the American cop show *Starsky & Hutch*. The best thing was the car that the two cops drove. It was a red Ford Torino with a white stripe and nicknamed 'the striped tomato'.

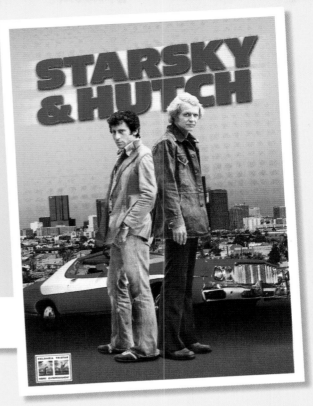

You can see Starsky and Hutch's famous red and white car in the background of this picture.

Top books of the time were Roald Dahl's *Charlie and the Chocolate Factory* and Richard Adams' *Watership Down*. *Watership Down* told the story of a band of rabbits and was read by adults as well as teenagers. Books that had been written by Enid Blyton in the 1940s, '50s and '60s remained favourites with many children. In the '70s, her *Famous Five* stories were made into a TV series.

Peter asks his aunt what she liked to read:

I loved horses and enjoyed watching *The Adventures of Black Beauty* on TV. That got me reading *Black Beauty*, the **novel** it was based on. I liked the Enid Blyton books too and loved reading about the adventures of the Famous Five.

Here is a 1970s edition of one of Enid Blyton's *Famous Five* novels. The books told the adventures of a group of children, Dick, Julian, Anne and George (short for Georgina), and their dog Timmy.

From glam rock to punk

The new music of the early '70s was 'glam rock'. The name was used for artists such as David Bowie and Elton John as well as bands like Slade and T-Rex. They all wore flashy outfits, often with lots of glitter.

Marc Bolan, the lead singer of glam rock band T-Rex often wore colourful clothes and make-up. Lots of people copied the way he dressed.

Alice asks her mother what music she liked:
I liked glam rock bands and had a big poster of Marc Bolan from T-Rex on my bedroom wall. I was also a fan of a Scottish teenage band called the Bay City Rollers. I copied the way they dressed by shortening my jeans and sewing tartan to the bottom edges.

Reggae music from Jamaica and **funk** from the USA were both popular, while disco music was at its **peak**. The Bee Gees' album *Saturday Night Fever* featured songs from the movie and became one of the best-selling albums of all time. Swedish pop band Abba had lots of hits.

Swedish band Abba became world famous after winning the Eurovision Song Contest in 1974.

Sarah asks her father about pop music:

I couldn't wait for Thursdays when *Top of the Pops* on the TV played music from the charts, and I always listened to Radio 1 on Sunday evenings to hear DJ Alan 'Fluff' Freeman tell us who was 'number one'.

In 1976, a new, harsher style of rock music called punk appeared. The leading British punk bands were the Sex Pistols and The Clash. Some of these bands aimed to shock with their songs, appearance and behaviour.

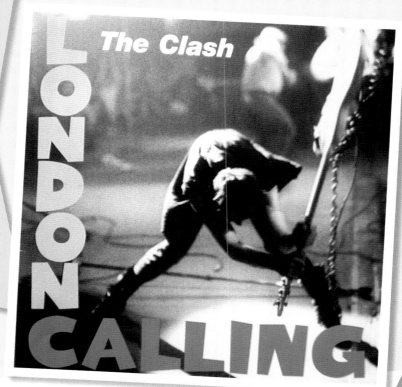

Punk rock band The Clash formed in 1976. This famous album cover shows a band member about to smash his guitar!

Fashions

At the beginning of the '70s, girls wore both maxi (very long) and mini skirts. They also wore very short shorts called 'hotpants'. Both sexes wore very flared trousers and clumpy platform shoes or clogs.

Fashion was closely linked to music, and glam rock brought its own style. This meant wearing lots of glitter, satin, silver and make-up. Three-piece suits with matching trousers, jackets and waistcoats became popular with men and women. Wide ties, called 'kipper ties' were also fashionable.

This is a photo of Hazel's father, Paul (second from the left) taken in 1976 when long hair and flared jeans were still in fashion.

Hazel's mother remembers:

I remember going to a school disco wearing red satin shorts that were very fashionable in the late '70s. My mum is a brilliant dressmaker and she made them for me. They were really fab. This photo was taken when she and my stepfather got married. Mum made the capes that me and my older sister, Fiona, are wearing.

Matty asks his aunt about hairstyles:

For a time I wore my hair flicked back in the 'Farah flick'. It was a style made popular by the actress Farah Fawcett in the TV show *Charlie's Angels*. To get the style you had to use electric curling tongs once or twice a day.

Here is a picture of Karen in a stripy top with her family in the early '70s. Her mother and aunt have short, layered hairstyles that were very popular at the time.

Alice asks her mother what she used to wear:

I made lots of my own clothes, including a three-piece suit. The trousers, waistcoat and jacket were all made out of chocolate brown velvet.

Later on there was the punk look, with spikey bleached or brightly-coloured hair, dark make-up and ripped clothes held together with safety pins. Some punks wore safety pins through their cheeks or below the eyebrow!

A group of punks in London's fashionable King's Road in 1979.

Schooldays

In 1972, the school leaving age was raised from 15 to 16. Methods of teaching were changing. Instead of sitting in rows of desks, children began working together in groups and teachers helped them to find out information for themselves.

This picture of a primary school classroom taken in 1971 shows children working together in groups.

Matty asks his aunt what school was like:

My primary school was a modern building with big classrooms. We sat together at large tables for group work, but always with a good view of the blackboard. I was very happy there. When we were studying Elizabethan life in history, we learned an Elizabethan dance that we performed on stage for the parents. In this photo of the dance, I'm the fifth from the left in the white and gold costume.

Matty's aunt at primary school.

Today, schoolchildren across the country study many of the same subjects. Things were different in the '70s when schools were free to choose most of the subjects they taught.

22

Children enjoy a school dinner of fish fingers, baked beans and potato followed by sponge pudding and custard.

All schools provided hot meals for children at lunchtime. Children paid for the meals but those from the poorest families had them free. Physical punishment such as caning was still allowed, but many schools stopped using it in the '70s.

Sarah asks her father what he remembers about school:

I used to have hot school dinners. The dinner ladies could be a bit bossy and they would sometimes say you couldn't have any pudding until you had finished your main course.

Hazel asks her father about his schooldays:

I didn't like going to secondary school much. I was a bit cheeky so I got all the different types of punishment, including beatings with a rubber strap and a cane. I was really fed up when the leaving age was raised to 16.

At work

Through the 1970s, workers fought for higher wages by going on strike. The strikes led to **shortages** of all kinds, including power. In 1973, the government cut the working week to just three days to save electricity. During the winter of 1978-79 strikes forced hospitals and schools to close.

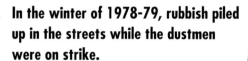

In the winter of 1978-79, rubbish piled up in the streets while the dustmen were on strike.

British goods were becoming more expensive to produce and buy, so people began buying cheaper foreign goods instead. Many factories had to close down. By the late '70s, about 1.5 million people in Britain were **unemployed**.

Hazel asks her father about the strikes:

I remember the miners' strikes, the three-day weeks and power cuts. It was a tough time for my family. Dad worked on a coal lorry and the number of hours he worked was cut. We were very short of money.

Alice asks her mother about working in the '70s:
My parents didn't want me to follow in their footsteps and go into farming. They thought farming was getting too difficult. A lot of people were out of work and claiming money from the government. In 1978 I got a job with social services to check that people were claiming money honestly.

There were improvements for working women. In 1970, the Equal Pay Act made it **illegal** to pay women less than men for doing the same job. Then in 1975, another law made it illegal for employers to refuse women jobs just because they were women. By the end of the '70s the number of women going out to work had risen to 65 per cent from 55 per cent at the beginning of the decade.

This is Barbara Castle, the politician who introduced the Equal Pay Act of 1970.

In the 1970s, new laws gave women more equality with men in the workplace. This picture shows a team of women at work in a police headquarters.

Getting about

By the 1970s, half of all households had a car, compared to 30 per cent at the start of the '60s. The network of motorways continued to grow. The British-built Ford Cortina was the best-selling British car of the '70s. The Ford Capri was a popular sporty model.

A 1973 Ford Capri. This bright yellow was a favourite colour for cars at that time.

Alice asks her mother how she travelled:

We lived on a farm until 1979 and I needed my own transport to get about. I had a moped [a low-powered motorcycle] when I was 16 and then when I was a bit older I got my own car. It was a small Fiat 126 – a popular car in the '70s. It had the engine in the back and made a 'phut-phutting' noise.

Hazel asks her father what type of car his parents had:

My parents had an old Hillman Imp which was tiny but had a fabulous back window that opened upwards. It didn't like going up hills so we often had to take a longer route to avoid them. The headlights were a bit dim too. When there was thick fog, my dad used to walk in front of it with a torch!

Alice's mum drove a Fiat 126 like this one.

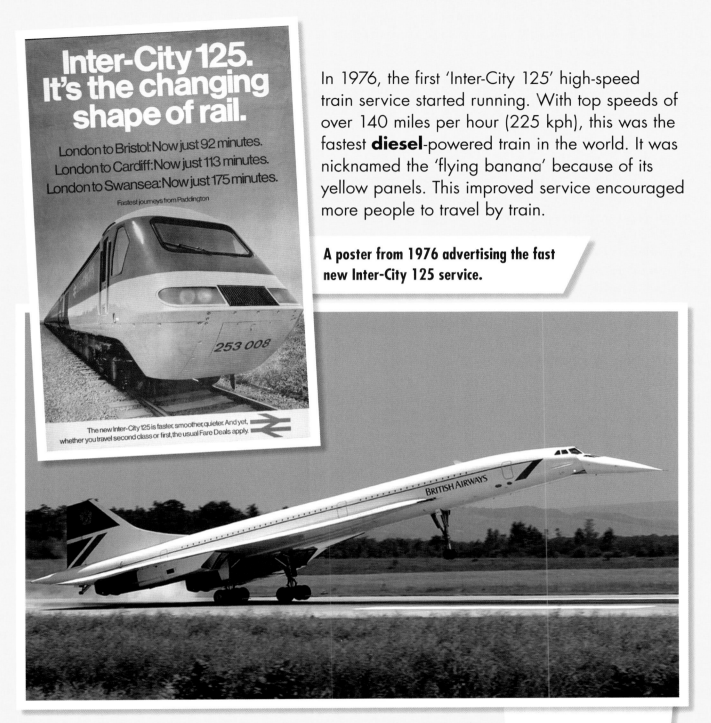

Inter-City 125.
It's the changing
shape of rail.

London to Bristol: Now just 92 minutes.
London to Cardiff: Now just 113 minutes.
London to Swansea: Now just 175 minutes.

Fastest journeys from Paddington

253 008

The new Inter-City 125 is faster, smoother, quieter. And yet,
whether you travel second class or first, the usual Fare Deals apply.

In 1976, the first 'Inter-City 125' high-speed train service started running. With top speeds of over 140 miles per hour (225 kph), this was the fastest **diesel**-powered train in the world. It was nicknamed the 'flying banana' because of its yellow panels. This improved service encouraged more people to travel by train.

A poster from 1976 advertising the fast new Inter-City 125 service.

BRITISH AIRWAYS

In 1970, the first Boeing 747 service began. These huge 'Jumbo' jets could carry twice as many people as ordinary jet liners and made airfares cheaper. Concorde (above) started making passenger flights in 1976. It could cross the **Atlantic** in just 3 hours, but the fares were very expensive.

Concorde was famous for its high speed and beauty. Because of its beak-like nose, some called it 'the big bird'.

Holiday time

As air travel became cheaper, seaside holidays in the UK became less popular. More people could afford holidays abroad where they could be sure of sunny weather. Spain, France and Greece were favourite holiday destinations. Lots of people went on **package holidays** where travel and accommodation were included in the price.

The Spanish holiday resort of Benidorm attracted lots of holidaymakers in the 1970s. Many high-rise hotels were quickly built to provide accommodation.

Sarah asks her mother about holidays:

My mother was from Jamaica and in 1974 we went there on holiday. It was the first time she'd been back to Jamaica since the 1950s. We flew with Jamaican Airways and the whole thing was so exciting. I remember thinking that it must have been very hard for my mum to leave such a beautiful place.

TIME DIFFERENCE

In 1971, people in the UK made 6.7 million holiday trips abroad. In 2009, there were 43 million holiday trips abroad.

Back in the UK, lots of people with their own cars were going camping or caravanning. These types of holiday gave holidaymakers much more freedom than staying in hotels or **guesthouses**.

Hazel asks her dad what his holidays were like:

My family and I used to visit my grandma's caravan near Skegness. We also had a few holidays at my Uncle Doug's place in Tenby, Wales. It used to take us all day to get there in our little car so it felt a bit like going abroad!

A British beach holiday in the hot summer of 1976.

Hazel's father (right) on holiday near Skegness in the early '70s.

Hazel asks her mother where she went on holiday:

We used to rent a cottage in the summer holidays, either near a beach or in the countryside. We'd drive off in the car with suitcases covered in plastic and strapped onto the roof rack. It was a really big deal when we went abroad to Greece one year. I also went on some school trips to France and Amsterdam that were full of adventures.

Hazel's mother Abigail on a school trip to France in 1978.

Find out what your family remembers

Try asking members of your family what they remember about the 1970s. You could ask them the same questions that children in this book have asked and then compare the answers you get. Ask your relatives how they think that life in the '70s was different from today. Get them to talk about their favourite memories or important events of the time. This will help you build up your own picture of life in the 1970s. It will also help you find out more about your family history.

These stamps marked Britain joining the European Economic Community (now called the European Union).

Timeline

1970 The age at which the law recognises young people as adults is lowered from 21 to 18. The Boeing 747 'Jumbo' jet goes into service. The Equal Pay Act gives women the same right to pay as men.

1971 Britain changes to decimal currency.

1972 Coal miners go on strike for seven weeks. School leaving age raised from 15 to 16.

1973 The government introduces the three-day week to save power. Britain becomes part of the **EEC (now the European Union).**

1975 The Sex Discrimination Act makes it illegal to refuse a woman a job because of her sex.

1976 The first Inter-City 125 train goes into service. Concorde, the plane that can travel at twice the speed of sound, goes into service. Britain has the hottest summer for 200 years.

1977 The Queen's Silver Jubilee marks 25 years of her reign. Punk band the Sex Pistols have a hit with *God Save the Queen*. The film *Star Wars* is released.

1978 VHS video recorders go on sale.

1978–79 Over the autumn and winter months, strikes cause chaos across the country.

1979 Margaret Thatcher, the leader of the Conservative Party, becomes Britain's first woman prime minister.

Glossary

animations
When a series of drawings or photographs of puppets or models is filmed to make them appear to move.

Atlantic
The world's second largest ocean, separating North and South America from Europe and Africa.

blockbuster
A film, play or book that has enormous success.

bomb scare
When people have to leave a building or area because there may be a bomb there.

convenience food
Food that can be prepared quickly and easily.

decimal
Based on the number 10.

diesel
A heavy oil used as fuel.

EEC (now the European Union)
A group of European countries set up to help each other and make trade easier between its members.

funk
A type of dance music started by African American musicians in the late 1960s.

guesthouse
A private home that offers accommodation to paying guests.

illegal
Against the law.

novel
A book with a plot and different characters that tells a long story.

package holidays
Holidays organised by travel agents that include travel and accommodation in the price.

peak
A period where something is at its highest point or at its most popular.

power cut
When the electricity supply to an area stops.

punk
A style or type of music from the 1970s that was rebellious and often shocked people.

reggae
A Jamaican style of music with a strong beat.

reign
The period during which a king or queen is on the throne.

science fiction
Books, films, television programmes or plays that use science in an imaginative way and are often set in the future.

shagpile carpet
Carpet with long, thick fibres.

shilling
A silver coin that was equal to 12 old pennies and worth 5p in today's money.

shortage
When there is a lack or not enough of something.

Silver Jubilee
A celebration marking 25 years of a king or queen being on the throne.

strikes
When workers refuse to work because of a dispute, often over pay or working conditions.

Troubles
The name given to a period of violence in Northern Ireland which spilled into other parts of the UK and lasted for 30 years from the late 1960s.

unemployed
Without a job.

Further information

Books:

Home Life (Britain Since 1948), by Neil Tonge, Wayland, 2008
The 1970s (I Can Remember), by Sally Hewitt, Franklin Watts, 2003
The 1970s from Watergate to Disco (Decades of the 20th Century in Color), by Stephen Feinstein, Enslow Publishers, 2006
1960s and 1970s (Children in History), by Kate Jackson Bedford, Franklin Watts, 2009

Websites:

For a general outline of the 1970s with links to other websites, try
http://primaryhomeworkhelp.co.uk/war/1970s.html
This BBC website has lots of memories from people who grew up in the 1970s
http://news.bbc.co.uk/1/hi/magazine/decades/1970s/

Index